W9-CEC-192

The Big Book of
God's Little Instructions

HONOR
BOOKS

Tulsa, Oklahoma

The Big Book of God's Little Instructions
ISBN 1-56292-147-9
Copyright © 1996 by Honor Books, Inc.
P.O. Box 55388
Tulsa, Oklahoma 74155

Printed in the United States of America. All rights reserved under International Copyright Law. Contents and/or cover may not be reproduced in whole or in part in any form without the express written consent of the Publisher.

Introduction

The Big Book of God's Little Instructions is a collection of the best of the best quotes and scriptures from the entire God's Little Instruction Book Series. All of these books were designed to be fun to read, yet thought-provoking. The quotes and scriptures will inspire you to strive for excellence and character in living, and many will lift your spirits with a good laugh. There is something for everyone in this unusual compilation, touching every area of life.

In keeping with our pledge to publish encouraging, inspiring, and motivating books for your enjoyment, we hope you will treasure and enjoy this special collection.

I have never been hurt by anything I didn't say.

Don't talk so much. You keep putting your foot in your mouth. Be sensible and turn off the flow!
Proverbs 10:19 TLB

Marriage should be honored by all, and the marriage bed kept pure, for God will judge the adulterer and all the sexually immoral.

Hebrews 13:4 NIV

The Bible has a word to describe "safe" sex: it's called marriage.

Opportunities are seldom labeled.

Seek, and ye shall find; knock, and it shall be opened unto you.
Matthew 7:7

When I was a child, I spake as a child, I understood as a child, I thought as a child: but when I became a man, I put away childish things.
1 Corinthians 13:11

Maturity doesn't come with age; it comes with acceptance of responsibility.

I am only one;
but still I am one.
I cannot do every-
thing, but still I can
do something; I will
not refuse to do the
something I can do.

*Under his
(Christ's) direction
the whole body is
fitted together
perfectly, and each
part in its own
special way helps
the other parts.*
Ephesians 4:16 TLB

For the vision is yet for an appointed time...it will surely come, it will not tarry.

Habakkuk 2:3

The future belongs to those who see possibilities before they become obvious.

It needs more skill
than I can tell
to play the second
fiddle well.

*But he that is
greatest among
you shall be
your servant.
Matthew 23:11*

We do not want you to become lazy, but to imitate those who through faith and patience inherit what has been promised.

Hebrews 6:12 NIV

Everything comes to him who hustles while he waits.

Kites rise highest against the wind, not with it.

For when the way is rough, your patience has a chance to grow. So let it grow, and don't try to squirm out of your problems.
James 1:3-4 TLB

So Peter....walked on the water toward Jesus. But when he looked around at the high waves, he was terrified and began to sink.
Matthew 14:29-30 TLB

Obstacles are those frightful things you see when you take your eyes off the goal.

Hating people is
like burning down
your own house
to get rid of a rat.

*But if ye bite
and devour one
another, take heed
that ye be not
consumed one
of another.*
Galatians 5:15

The ear that heareth the reproof of life abideth among the wise.

Proverbs 15:31

A good listener is not only popular everywhere, but after a while he knows something.

Give me a task too big, too hard for human hands, then I shall come at length to lean on thee, and leaning, find my strength.

Trust in the Lord with all your heart and lean not on your own understanding.
Proverbs 3:5 NIV

Can two walk together, except they be agreed?

Amos 3:3

Success is knowing the difference between cornering people and getting them in your corner.

Shoot for the moon.
Even if you miss it
you will land
among the stars.

Aim for perfection.
2 Corinthians
13:11 NIV

But they do all their deeds to be noticed by men.
Matthew 23:5
NASB

Definition of status: Buying something you don't need with money you don't have to impress people you don't like.

I like the dreams of the future better than the history of the past.

Remember ye not the former things, neither consider the things of old. Behold, I will do a new thing.
Isaiah 43:18-19

It is senseless to pay tuition to educate a rebel who has no heart for truth.

Proverbs 17:16

TLB

You can lead a boy to college, but you cannot make him think.

Nothing great was ever achieved without enthusiasm.

For the joy of the Lord is your strength.
Nehemiah 8:10

Though your beginning was insignificant, Yet your end will increase greatly.

Job 8:7 NASB

Don't be discouraged; everyone who got where he is, started where he was.

He that has learned to obey will know how to command.

The wise in heart accept commands, but a chattering fool comes to ruin.
Proverbs 10:8 NIV

In the multitude of words there wanteth not sin: but he that refraineth his lips is wise.

Proverbs 10:19

The most valuable of all talents is that of never using two words when one will do.

The greatest use of life is to spend it for something that will outlast it.

But store up for yourselves treasures in heaven, where moth and rust do not destroy, and where thieves do not break in and steal.
Matthew 6:20 NIV

Reaching forth unto those things which are before, I press toward the mark for the prize of the high calling of God in Christ Jesus.

Philippians 3:13-14

Unless you try to do something beyond what you have already mastered, you will never grow.

Money is a good servant but a bad master.

The rich ruleth the poor, and the borrower is servant to the lender.
Proverbs 22:7

He who heeds discipline shows the way to life, but whoever ignores correction leads others astray.

Proverbs 10:17 NIV

An error doesn't become a mistake until you refuse to correct it.

30

The difference between the right word and the almost right word is the difference between lightning and the lightning bug.

A word fitly spoken is like apples of gold in pictures of silver.
Proverbs 25:11

Not only to say the right thing in the right place, but far more difficult, to leave unsaid the wrong thing at the tempting moment.

Self-control means controlling the tongue! A quick retort can ruin everything.

Proverbs 13:3 TLB

The road to success is dotted with many tempting parking places.

Let us lay aside every weight, and the sin which doth so easily beset us, and let us run with patience the race that is set before us.

Hebrews 12:1

Husbands, love your wives, as Christ loved the church and gave Himself up for her.
Ephesians 5:25
AMP

The most important thing a father can do for his children is to love their mother.

A house is made of walls and beams; a home is made of love and dreams.

She looks well to the ways of her household, And does not eat the bread of idleness.

Proverbs 31:27

NASB

When angry, do not sin; do not ever let your wrath — your exasperation, your fury or indignation — last until the sun goes down.
Ephesians 4:26
AMP

An argument is the longest distance between two points.

The best way for you and your spouse to guarantee some time without the kids is to do the dinner dishes together.

Two can accomplish more than twice as much as one, for the results can be much better.
Ecclesiastes 4:9 TLB

And though a man might prevail against one who is alone, two will withstand him. A threefold cord is not quickly broken.

Ecclesiastes 4:12

RSV

The closer a man and his wife get to Christ, the clearer they see how important it is for them to stay close to each other.

A wise lover values not so much the gift of the lover as the love of the giver.

How fair is thy love, my sister, my spouse! how much better is thy love than wine! and the smell of thine ointments than all spices!
Song of Solomon 4:10

And be kind to one another, tenderhearted, forgiving one another, even as God in Christ forgave you.
Ephesians 4:32
NKJV

A happy marriage is the union of two good forgivers.

The bonds of matrimony are worthless unless the interest is kept up.

Live happily with the woman you love through the fleeting days of life, for the wife God gives you is your best reward down here for all your earthly toil.

Ecclesiastes 9:9 TLB

Nevertheless let each one of you in particular so love his own wife as himself, and let the wife see that she respects her husband.

Ephesians 5:33

NKJV

Marriage may be inspired by music, soft words, and perfume; but its security is manifest in work, consideration, respect, and well-fried bacon.

Many parents are
finding out that
a pat on the back
helps develop
character — if
given often enough,
early enough,
and low enough.

*Correct your son,
and he will give
you rest; Yes, he
will give delight
to your soul.
Proverbs 29:17
NKJV*

To keep your marriage brimming, with love in the loving cup, whenever you're wrong, admit it, whenever you're right, shut up.

Confess to one another therefore your faults... and pray [also] for one another, that you may be healed and restored.
James 5:16 AMP

Marriage is a marathon, not a sprint.

And Jacob served seven years for Rachel; and they seemed unto him but a few days, for the love he had to her.
Genesis 29:20

Listen to advice and accept instruction, and in the end you will be wise.

Proverbs 19:20

NIV

Good listeners make good lovers.

Children don't divide a couple's love — they multiply it.

~

Children are a gift from God; they are his reward.
Psalm 127:3 TLB

Death and life are in the power of the tongue: and they that love it shall eat the fruit thereof.

Proverbs 18:21

You can send your marriage to an early grave with a series of little digs.

Being married teaches us at least one very valuable lesson — to think before we speak.

A word aptly spoken is like apples of gold in settings of silver.
Proverbs 25:11 NIV

Give, and it will be given to you. A good measure, pressed down, shaken together and running over, will be poured into your lap. For with the measure you use, it will be measured to you.

Luke 6:38 NIV

Love is the one business in which it pays to be an absolute spendthrift: Give it away; throw it away; splash it over; empty your pockets; shake the basket; and tomorrow you'll have more than ever.

Love is being willing to face risks to see your spouse's dreams come true.

This is how we know what love is: Jesus Christ laid down his life for us. And we ought to lay down our lives for our brothers.
1 John 3:16 NIV

Be patient with each other, making allowance for each other's faults because of your love.
Ephesians 4:2 TLB

A loving spouse can see the good in you even when you can't.

Give your troubles to God; He will be up all night anyway.

Casting all your anxiety upon Him, because He cares for you.
1 Peter 5:7 NASB

You will be happy and it will be well with you. Your wife shall be like a fruitful vine, Within your house, Your children like olive plants Around your table.

Psalm 128:2-3

NASB

Love makes a house a home.

We should seize every opportunity to give encouragement. Encouragement is oxygen to the soul.

But encourage one another daily, as long as it is called Today.
Hebrews 3:13 NIV

Practice what you have learned and received and heard and seen in me, and model your way of living on it, and the God of peace — of untroubled, undisturbed well-being — will be with you.

Philippians 4:9

AMP

A marriage may be made in heaven, but the maintenance must be done on earth.

Sharing the
housework
makes it easier
to share the love.

*Bear one another's
burdens, and
so fulfil the law
of Christ.*
Galatians 6:2 RSV

I will betroth you to me forever; I will betroth you in righteousness and justice, in love and compassion.

Hosea 2:19 NIV

A successful marriage requires falling in love many times, always with the same person.

Love is friendship set on fire.

Many waters cannot quench love, neither can floods drown it.
Song of Solomon 8:7 *RSV*

But that as a matter of equality your abundance at the present time should supply their want, so that their abundance may supply your want, that there may be equality.
2 Corinthians 8:14 RSV

Love's lasting comes in erasing the boundary line between "mine" and "yours."

Marriage is a promise that is shared by only two — a vow to love and dream and plan together all life through.

If two of you on earth agree (harmonize together, together make a symphony) about — anything and everything — whatever they shall ask, it will come to pass and be done for them.
Matthew 18:19
AMP

A man shall leave his father and mother and be joined to his wife, and the two shall become one flesh.
Ephesians 5:31
NKJV

Two souls with but a single thought, two hearts that beat as one.

Spouses who put their partners first have marriages that last.

But in lowliness of mind let each esteem other better than themselves.
Philippians 2:3

Submitting yourselves one to another in the fear of God. Ephesians 5:21

Successful marriages usually rest on a foundation of accountability between husbands and wives.

Let the wife make the husband glad to come home, and let him make her sorry to see him leave.

Let each man of you (without exception) love his wife as [being in a sense] his very own self; and let the wife see that she respects and reveres her husband — that she notices him, regards him...

Ephesians 5:33

AMP

If thou faint in the day of adversity, thy strength is small.

Proverbs 24:10

The difference between smooth sailing and shipwreck in marriage lies in what you as a couple are doing about the rough weather.

Marriage is like harmony: two sets of notes for the same song.

Complete my joy by being of the same mind, having the same love, being in full accord and of one mind.
Philippians 2:2
RSV

Therefore encourage one another, and build up one another.
1 Thessalonians 5:11 NASB

The most successful marriages are those where both the husband and the wife seek to build the self-esteem of the other.

A child is not likely to find a father in God unless he finds something of God in his father.

Be ye followers of me, even as I also am of Christ.
I Corinthians 11:1

Let this mind be in you, which was also in Christ Jesus:...(who) took upon him the form of a servant.
Philippians 2:5,7

My primary role is not to be the boss and just look good but to be a servant leader who enables and enhances my family to be their best.

Honor is better than honors.

For them that honour me I will honour.
1 Samuel 2:30

Withhold not good from them to whom it is due, when it is in the power of thine hand to do it.

Proverbs 3:27

It may be hard on some fathers not to have a son, but it is much harder on a boy not to have a father.

One hundred years from now it won't matter if you got that big break,...or finally traded up to a Mercedes. It will greatly matter, one hundred years from now, that you made a commitment to Jesus Christ.

For what is a man profited, if he shall gain the whole world, and lose his own soul?
Matthew 16:26

Don't be fools;
be wise: make
the most of every
opportunity
you have for
doing good.
Ephesians 5:16
TLB

Children spell "love"...T-I-M-E.

It is better to bind your children to you by a feeling of respect, and by gentleness, than by fear.

Thy gentleness hath made me great.
Psalm 18:35

You can't do much about your ancestors but you can influence your descendants enormously.

But as for me and my house, we will serve the Lord.
Joshua 24:15

By profession I am a soldier and take pride in that fact, but I am prouder to be a father.

I have great confidence in you; I take great pride in you.
2 Corinthians 7:4
NIV

Death and life are in the power of the tongue: and they that love it shall eat the fruit thereof.
Proverbs 18:21

We can either grace our children, or damn them with unrequited wounds which never seem to heal...men, as fathers you have such power!

Dad, when you come home at night with only shattered pieces of your dreams, your little one can mend them like new with two magic words — "Hi, Dad!"

For we have great joy and consolation in thy love.
Philemon 7

Iron sharpeneth iron; so a man sharpeneth the countenance of his friend.

Proverbs 27:17

Keep company with good men and good men you will imitate.

My father is the
standard by which
all subsequent
men in my life
have been judged.

*Leaving us an
example, that
ye should follow
his steps.*
1 Peter 2:21

Children miss nothing in sizing up their parents. If you are only half convinced of your beliefs, they will quickly discern that fact.

Let us hold fast the profession of our faith without wavering.

Hebrews 10:23

If a man cannot be a Christian in the place where he is, he cannot be a Christian anywhere.

Let your light so shine before men, that they may see your good works, and glorify your Father which is in heaven.

Matthew 5:16

Therefore be imitators of God, as beloved children; and walk in love, just as Christ also loved you, and gave Himself up for us, an offering and a sacrifice to God as a fragrant aroma.

Ephesians 5:1-2

NASB

Children need love, especially when they do not deserve it.

The strength of a man consists in finding out the way God is going, and going that way.

I am the light of the world: he that followeth me shall not walk in darkness, but shall have the light of life.

John 8:12

A child's glory is his father.
Proverbs 17:6 TLB

There are many ways to measure success; not the least of which is the way your child describes you when talking to a friend.

If you want your child to accept your values when he reaches his teen years, then you must be worthy of his respect during his younger days.

...a model for you, that you might follow our example.
2 Thessalonians 3:9 NASB

Death and life are in the power of the tongue: and they that love it shall eat the fruit thereof.

Proverbs 18:21

A father's words are like a thermostat that sets the temperature in the house.

Too much love never spoils children. Children become spoiled when we substitute "presents" for "presence."

We loved you dearly — so dearly that we gave you not only God's message, but our own lives too.
1 Thessalonians 2:8 TLB

Those things, which ye have both learned, and received, and heard, and seen in me, do: and the God of peace shall be with you.

Philippians 4:9

For many little girls, life with father is a dress rehearsal for love and marriage.

You cannot teach a child to take care of himself unless you will let him try...He will make mistakes; and out of these mistakes will come his wisdom.

And all thy children shall be taught of the Lord; and great shall be the peace of thy children.
Isaiah 54:13

When we love something it is of value to us, and when something is of value to us we spend time with it, time enjoying it and time taking care of it.

And I will very gladly spend and be spent for you.
2 Corinthians
12:15

Nothing I've ever done has given me more joys and rewards than being a father to my children.

Lo, children are an heritage of the Lord; and the fruit of the womb is his reward.

Psalm 127:3

Fathers,...do not be hard on them (children) or harass them; lest they become discouraged.
Colossians 3:21
AMP

Children are like clocks; they must be allowed to run.

Performance under stress is one test of effective leadership. It may also be the proof of accomplishment when it comes to evaluating the quality of a father.

Cast thy burden upon the Lord, and he shall sustain thee: he shall never suffer the righteous to be moved.
Psalm 55:22

Withhold not correction from the child: for if thou beatest him with the rod, he shall not die. Thou shalt beat him with the rod, and shalt deliver his soul from hell.
Proverbs 23: 13-14

Many a man spanks his children for things his own father should have spanked him for.

Opportunities for meaningful communication between fathers and sons must be created. And it's work to achieve.

To everything there is a season,...a time to keep silence, and a time to speak.
Ecclesiastes 3:1,7

And he shall turn the heart of the fathers to the children, and the heart of the children to their fathers.
Malachi 4:6

The great man is he who does not lose his child's heart.

Unless a father accepts his faults he will most certainly doubt his virtues.

He hath made us accepted in the beloved.
Ephesians 1:6

There is a right time for everything: A time to laugh... Ecclesiastes 3:1,4 TLB

Fathers are what give daughters away to other men who aren't nearly good enough ...so they can have grandchildren that are smarter than anybody's.

When I was a boy of fourteen my father was so ignorant I could hardly stand to have the old man around. But when I got to be twenty-one I was astonished at how much the old man had learned in seven years.

There is a right time for everything: A time to laugh...
Ecclesiastes 3:1,4
TLB

A merry heart doeth good like a medicine.
Proverbs 17:22

A father is a person who is forced to endure childbirth without an anesthetic.

Character is not made in crisis, it is only exhibited.

I have set the Lord always before me: because he is at my right hand, I shall not be moved.

Psalm 16:8

I would have you learn this great fact: that a life of doing right is the wisest life there is. If you live that kind of life, you'll not limp or stumble as you run.

Proverbs 4:11,12 TLB

Wisdom is the quality that keeps you from getting into situations where you need it.

Depend on it, God's work done in God's way will never lack God's supplies.

If you are willing and obedient, you will eat the best from the land.
Isaiah 1:19 NIV

If you profit from constructive criticism you will be elected to the wise men's hall of fame. But to reject criticism is to harm yourself and your own best interest.

Proverbs 15:31-32

TLB

The trouble with most of us is that we would rather be ruined by praise than saved by criticism.

Life affords no greater responsibility, no greater privilege, than the raising of the next generation.

Teach them (God's commandments) to your children, talking about them when you sit at home and when you walk along the road, when you lie down and when you get up. So that your days and the days of your children may be many.

Deuteronomy 11:19,21 NIV

He who restrains his lips is wise.

Proverbs 10:19

NASB

Smart people speak from experience — smarter people from experience, don't speak.

I've suffered a great many catastrophes in my life. Most of them never happened.

For God hath not given us the spirit of fear; but of power, and of love, and of a sound mind.

2 Timothy 1:7

Little children, let us stop just saying we love people; let us really love them, and show it by our actions.
1 John 3:18 TLB

What a big difference there is between giving advice and lending a hand.

The man who pays an ounce of principle for a pound of popularity gets badly cheated.

For they loved the praise of men more than the praise of God.
John 12:43

Let your character or moral disposition be free from love of money — [including] greed, avarice, lust, and craving for earthly possessions — and be satisfied with your present [circumstances and with what you have].

Hebrews 13:5 AMP

If the grass looks greener on the other side of the fence, you can bet the water bill is higher.

Some people reach the top of the ladder of success only to find it is leaning against the wrong wall.

But seek ye first the kingdom of God, and his righteousness; and all these things shall be added unto you.
Matthew 6:33

Happy is that people...whose God is the Lord.
Psalm 144:15

The happiness of every country depends upon the character of its people, rather than the form of its government.

The only way to have a friend is to be one.

A man that hath friends must shew himself friendly.
Proverbs 18:24

Let another man praise thee, and not thine own mouth; a stranger, and not thine own lips.

Proverbs 27:2

The man who sings his own praises always gets the wrong pitch.

Our faith should be our steering wheel not our spare tire.

But the righteous will live by his faith.
Habakkuk 2:4 NIV

Lord, who may dwell in your sanctuary? He whose walk is blameless...who keeps his oath even when it hurts.
Psalm 15:1-2,4
NIV

A winner makes commitments; a loser makes promises.

It is reported that Moody's farewell words to his sons as he lay upon his deathbed were: "If God be your partner, make your plans large."

I can do all things through Christ which strengtheneth me.
Philippians 4:13

Faith doesn't make anything happen — faith rests on something that has happened!

My soul finds rest in God alone; my salvation comes from him.

Psalm 62:1 NIV

Choice, not chance, determines human destiny.

I have set before you life and death, blessing and cursing: therefore choose life, that both thou and thy seed may live.
Deuteronomy 30:19

Success is to be measured not so much by the position that one has reached in life as by the obstacles which he has overcome while trying to succeed.

Blessed is the man who perseveres under trial, because when he has stood the test, he will receive the crown of life that God has promised to those who love him.

James 1:12 NIV

To be upset over what you don't have is to waste what you do have.

Because the Lord is my Shepherd, I have everything I need!
Psalm 23:1 TLB

I warn everyone among you not to estimate and think of himself more highly than he ought — not to have an exaggerated opinion of his own importance.

Romans 12:3 AMP

Many a man thinks he has an open mind, when it's merely vacant.

Swallowing angry words before you say them is better than having to eat them afterwards.

From the fruit of his mouth a man's stomach is filled; with the harvest from his lips he is satisfied. The tongue has the power of life and death, and those who love it will eat its fruit.

Proverbs 18:20-21

NIV

And Jesus looking upon them saith, With men it is impossible, but not with God: for with God all things are possible.

Mark 10:27

God has a history of using the insignificant to accomplish the impossible.

It is not what a man does that determines whether his work is sacred or secular, it is why he does it.

Whatever you do, work at it with all your heart, as working for the Lord, not for men...It is the Lord Christ you are serving.
Colossians 3:23,24 NIV

For the value of wisdom is far above rubies; nothing can be compared with it.
Proverbs 8:11 TLB

Wisdom is the wealth of the wise.

Urgent things are seldom important. Important things are seldom urgent.

Every prudent man dealeth with knowledge.
Proverbs 13:16

My son, forget not my law; but let thine heart keep my commandments: So shalt thou find favour and good understanding in the sight of God and man.
Proverbs 3:1,4

People will be more impressed by the depth of your conviction than the height of your logic.

Life was a lot simpler when we honored father and mother rather than all the major credit cards.

Children, obey your parents in the Lord, for this is right. "Honor your father and mother" — which is the first commandment with a promise — "that it may go well with you and that you may enjoy long life on the earth." Ephesians 6:1-3 NIV

131

Whatsoever thy hand findeth to do, do it with thy might.

Ecclesiastes 9:10

Devoting a little of yourself to everything means committing a great deal of yourself to nothing.

Happiness is the result of circumstances, but joy endures in spite of circumstances.

In thy presence is fullness of joy; at thy right hand there are pleasures for evermore.
Psalm 16:11

*Offer to God
the sacrifice of
thanksgiving.
Psalm 50:14 AMP*

Some people are always grumbling because roses have thorns; I am thankful that thorns have roses.

Being at peace with yourself is a direct result of finding peace with God.

And the peace of God, which passeth all understanding, shall keep your hearts and mind through Christ Jesus.

Philippians 4:7

Uprightness and right standing with God [moral and spiritual rectitude in every area and relation] these elevate a nation, but sin is a reproach to any people.

Proverbs 14:34

AMP

A people that values its privileges above its principles soon loses both.

He who is waiting
for something to
turn up might
start with his
own shirt sleeves.

*All hard work
brings a profit,
but mere talk leads
only to poverty.*
Proverbs 14:23 NIV

Take fast hold of instruction; let her not go: keep her; for she is thy life.

Proverbs 4:13

If at first you don't succeed, try reading the instructions.

"No" is one of the few words that can never be misunderstood.

But let your statement be "Yes, yes" or "No, no".
Matthew 5:37 NASB

A man shall not be established by wickedness: but the root of the righteous shall not be moved.

Proverbs 12:3

The mighty oak was once a little nut that stood its ground.

Although the tongue weighs very little, few people are able to hold it.

Even so the tongue is a little member, and boasteth great things. Behold, how great a matter a little fire kindleth!

James 3:5

But thou, O man of God, flee these things; and follow after righteousness, godliness, faith, love, patience, meekness.

1 Timothy 6:11

Success in marriage is more than finding the right person. It's becoming the right person.

The trouble with the guy who talks too fast is that he often says something he hasn't thought of yet.

Be not rash with thy mouth, and let not thine heart be hasty to utter any thing before God: for God is in heaven, and thou upon earth: therefore let thy words be few.

Ecclesiastes 5:2

He also that is slothful in his work is brother to him that is a great waster.

Proverbs 18:9

Too many people quit looking for work when they find a job.

A shut mouth gathers no foot.

He that keepeth his mouth keepeth his life: but he that openeth wide his lips shall have destruction.

Proverbs 13:3

He that reproveth a scorner getteth to himself shame: and he that rebuketh a wicked man getteth himself a blot.

Proverbs 9:7

The only fool bigger than the person who knows it all is the person who argues with him.

The first step to wisdom is silence; the second is listening.

A wise man will hear, and will increase learning; and a man of understanding shall attain unto wise counsels.
Proverbs 1:5

But I say unto you, Love your enemies, bless them that curse you, do good to them that hate you, and pray for them which despitefully use you, and persecute you.

Matthew 5:44

Those who deserve love the least need it the most.

The best way to get even is to forget.

But love ye your enemies, and do good, and lend, hoping for nothing again; and your reward shall be great, and ye shall be the children of the Highest: for he is kind unto the unthankful and to the evil.

Luke 6:35

Work with your hands, just as we commanded you; so that you may behave properly toward outsiders and not be in any need.
1 Thessalonians 4:11-12 NASB

It takes more to plow a field than merely turning it over in your mind.

To forgive is to set a prisoner free and discover the prisoner was *you.*

For if ye forgive men their trespasses, your heavenly Father will also forgive you: But if ye forgive not men their trespasses, neither will your Father forgive your trespasses.
Matthew 6:14-15

The Lord seeth
not as man seeth;
for man looketh
on the outward
appearance, but
the Lord looketh
on the heart.

1 Samuel 16:7

When God measures
a man, He puts the
tape around the heart
instead of the head.

It is better to be silent and be considered a fool than to speak and remove all doubt.

Yea also, when he that is a fool walketh by the way, his wisdom faileth him, and he saith to every one that he is a fool.

Ecclesiastes 10:3

*If we are faithless,
He will remain
faithful, for he
cannot disown
himself.*
2 Timothy 2:13
NIV

Decisions can take you out of God's will but never out of His reach.

Patience is a quality you admire in the driver behind you and scorn in the one ahead.

The end of the matter is better than its beginning, and patience is better than pride. Do not be quickly provoked in your spirit, for anger resides in the lap of fools.
Ecclesiastes 7:8-9
NIV

Commit thy works unto the Lord, and thy thoughts shall be established.
Proverbs 16:3

The secret of achievement is to not let what you're doing get to you before you get to it.

Most people wish
to serve God —
but only in an
advisory capacity.

Humble yourselves
therefore under
the mighty hand
of God, that he
may exalt you
in due time.
1 Peter 5:6

A good man leaveth an inheritance to his children's children: and the wealth of the sinner is laid up for the just.

Proverbs 13:22

The measure of a man's character is not what he gets from his ancestors, but what he leaves his descendants.

The best bridge between hope and despair is often a good night's sleep.

It is vain for you to rise up early, to sit up late, to eat the bread of sorrows: for so he giveth his beloved sleep.
Psalm 127:2

He that is soon angry dealeth foolishly.
Proverbs 14:17

A man is never in worse company than when he flies into a rage and is beside himself.

Life can only be understood by looking backward, but it must be lived by looking forward.

And Jesus said unto him, No man, having put his hand to the plough, and looking back, is fit for the kingdom of God.
Luke 9:62

I will remember the works of the Lord: surely I will remember thy wonders of old. I will meditate also of all thy work, and talk of thy doings.

Psalm 77:11-12

Sometimes we are so busy adding up our troubles that we forget to count our blessings.

Authority makes some people grow — and others just swell.

But he that is greatest among you shall be your servant. And whosoever shall exalt himself shall be abased; and he that shall humble himself shall be exalted.
Matthew 23:11-12

If you have been trapped by what you said, ensnared by the words of your mouth, then do this, my son, to free yourself, since you have fallen into your neighbor's hands: Go and humble yourself; press your plea with your neighbor!
Proverbs 6:2-3
NIV

The best way to get the last word is to apologize.

The train of failure usually runs on the track of laziness.

By much slothfulness the building decayeth; and through idleness of the hands the house droppeth through.
Ecclesiastes 10:18

But godliness with contentment is great gain. For we brought nothing into this world, and it is certain we can carry nothing out.

1 Timothy 6:6-7

The secret of contentment is the realization that life is a gift not a right.

Those who bring sunshine to the lives of others cannot keep it from themselves.

Be not deceived; God is not mocked: for whatsoever a man soweth, that shall he also reap.
Galatians 6:7

And, ye fathers, provoke not your children to wrath: but bring them up in the nurture and admonition of the Lord.
Ephesians 6:4

No man ever really finds out what he believes in until he begins to instruct his children.

The best way to be successful is to follow the advice you give others.

He who ignores discipline despises himself, but whoever heeds correction gains understanding.
Proverbs 15:32 NIV

The righteousness of the blameless makes a straight way for them, but the wicked are brought down by their own wickedness.

Proverbs 11:5 NIV

Ability will enable a man to go to the top, but it takes character to keep him there.

God plus one is always a majority!

If God be for us, who can be against us?
Romans 8:31

Let every man be swift to hear, slow to speak, slow to wrath.

James 1:19

Ignorance is always swift to speak.

You don't have to lie awake nights to succeed — just stay awake days.

I must work the works of him that sent me, while it is day: the night cometh, when no man can work.

John 9:4

Your beauty should come from within you — the beauty of a gentle and quiet spirit. This beauty will never disappear, and it is worth very much to God.

1 Peter 3:4 ICB

Beauty shines through in the good that you do.

"**I**'m sorry, forgive me," are hard words to say. But when said from the heart they bring great joy your way.

But if we confess our sins, he will forgive our sins. We can trust God... He will make us clean from all the wrongs we have done.
1 John 1:9 ICB

Give, and you will receive. You will be given much....The way you give to others is the way God will give to you.
Luke 6:38 ICB

Hugs multiply when you give them away.

Take care to share.

Do not forget to do good to others. And share with them what you have.
Hebrews 13:16 ICB

You must not do wrong just because everyone else is doing it.
Exodus 23:2 ICB

Sin is what the serpent says is "in."

Sometimes we are asked to wait. But this we know — God's never late!

The Lord is good to those who put their hope in him. He is good to those who look to him for help. It is good to wait quietly for the Lord to save.

Lamentations 3:24-26 ICB

*Do for other
people the same
things you
want them to
do for you.
Matthew 7:12 ICB*

Whatever you say, whatever you do, bounces off others and comes back to you.

To delight
in the right,
makes you big
in God's sight.

*Those who want to
do right more than
anything else are
happy. God will
fully satisfy them.*
Matthew 5:6 ICB

Those who work to bring peace are happy. God will call them his sons.
Matthew 5:9 ICB

Increase the peace.

When brother's a bother and sister's sassy, pay them with patience.

Love is patient and kind.
1 Corinthians 13:4
ICB

If you forgive others for the things they do wrong, then your Father in heaven will also forgive you for the things you do wrong.

Matthew 6:14 ICB

When there's nothing to hide, you have peace inside.

Manners matter.

Love is not rude.
1 Corinthians 13:5
ICB

Give all your worries to him, because he cares for you.
1 Peter 5:7 ICB

Worry and frowns pull the heart down.

Don't quit or give up, when struggles you face. Those who keep trying will finish the race.

I keep trying to reach the goal and get the prize.
Philippians 3:14
ICB

The Father has loved us so much! He loved us so much that we are called children of God.
1 John 3:1 ICB

God loves you.

Faith is what you know is true. Faith is also what you do.

Faith that does nothing is worth nothing.
James 2:20 ICB

I praise you because you made me in an amazing and wonderful way.
Psalm 139:14 ICB

Snowflakes and fingerprints — you'll always find — each one is different, one of a kind. And just like a snowflake this, too, is true, no one else is exactly like you!

What you sow is what you grow.

A person harvests only what he plants.
Galatians 6:7 ICB

Be sure that no one pays back wrong for wrong.
1 Thessalonians 5:15 ICB

Two wrongs never make a right.

A smile never goes out of style.

Be full of joy in the Lord always.
Philippians 4:4 ICB

Think about the things that are good and worthy of praise.

Philippians 4:8

ICB

Good thoughts create sweet dreams.

Love listens.

We can come to God with no doubts. This means that when we ask God for things (and those things agree with what God wants for us), then God cares about what we say.

1 John 5:14 ICB

*God has poured
out his love to
fill our hearts.*
Romans 5:5 ICB

Find someone with a hole in their heart and fill it with God's love.

Problems are opportunities in disguise.

Those who were sad now are happy. God will comfort them.
Matthew 5:4 ICB

Those who are pure in their thinking are happy. They will be with God.

Matthew 5:8 ICB

The thoughts that you think are up to you, what you think is what you do.

An encouraging word deserves to be heard.

Say what people need — words that will help others become stronger.
Ephesians 4:29 ICB

The devil is always evil behind the "d."

Stand against the devil, and the devil will run away from you.
James 4:7 ICB

If you don't know, don't go!

Respect the Lord and refuse to do wrong.
Proverbs 3:7 ICB

I pray that the God who gives hope will fill you with much joy and peace while you trust in him.

Romans 15:13 ICB

Hope is something no one can ever take away from you. Only you can send it away.

Let your light shine.

In the same way, you should be a light for other people. Live so that they will see the good things you do. Live so that they will praise your Father in heaven.
Matthew 5:16 ICB

Always give thanks to God the Father for everything.
Ephesians 5:20
ICB

It's truly amazing just what they can do — those three little words, "please" and "thank you."

Helping hands make happy hearts.

Serve each other with love.
Galatians 5:13 ICB

*It is more blessed
to give than
to receive.*

Acts 20:35 ICB

Not what you get
but what you give,
determines the worth
of the life you live.

The secret of success is to do the common things uncommonly well.

Do you see a man skilled in his work? He will serve before kings; he will not serve before obscure men.

Proverbs 22:29 NIV

Do what is right and good in the sight of the Lord, so that it may go well with you.

Deuteronomy 6:18 NRSV

Efficiency is doing things right. Effectiveness is doing the right thing.

A great man is always willing to be little.

But the greatest among you shall be your servant.
Matthew 23:11
NASB

Stand at the crossroads and look; ask for the ancient paths, ask where the good way is, and walk in it, and you will find rest for your souls.

Jeremiah 6:16 NIV

Find out what you love to do and you will never have to work another day in your life.

The person who knows "how" will always have a job. The person who knows "why" will always be his boss.

How much better to get wisdom than gold! And to get understanding is to be chosen rather than silver.
Proverbs 16:16
NKJV

Therefore, take up the full armor of God, that you may be able to resist in the evil day, and having done everything, to stand firm. Stand firm therefore.

Ephesians 6:13-14

NASB

Courage is resistance to fear, mastery of fear. Not the absence of fear.

Some people succeed because they are destined to, but most people succeed because they are determined to.

Seest thou a man diligent in his business? He shall stand before kings.
Proverbs 22:29

Apply thine heart
unto instruction,
and thine ears
to the words
of knowledge.
Proverbs 23:12

A man who does not
read good books has
no advantage over
the man who can't
read them.

Triumph is just "umph" added to try.

And let us not be weary in well doing: for in due season we shall reap, if we faint not.

Galatians 6:9

So then, whether you eat or drink, or whatever you may do, do all for the honor and glory of God.

1 Corinthians 10:31 AMP

A great deal of good can be done in the world if one is not too careful who gets the credit.

Faith is daring the soul to go beyond what the eyes can see.

Now faith is the substance of things hoped for, the evidence of things not seen.
Hebrews 11:1 NKJV

Your ears shall hear a word behind you, saying, "This is the way, walk in it."
Isaiah 30:21 NKJV

Do not follow where the path may lead — go instead where there is no path and leave a trail.

Don't let your learning lead to knowledge, let your learning lead to action.

Be ye doers of the word, and not hearers only, deceiving your own selves.

James 1:22

His lord said unto him, Well done, thou good and faithful servant: thou hast been faithful over a few things, I will make thee ruler over many things.
Matthew 25:21

Don't let "Well done" on your tombstone mean you were cremated!

Genius is divine perseverance.

Having done all, to stand. Stand therefore.
Ephesians 6:13-14

*Be content
with such things
as ye have.*

Hebrews 13:5

The grass may look greener on the other side, but it still has to be mowed.

A man is not finished when he is defeated; he is finished when he quits.

And let us not be weary in well doing: for in due season we shall reap, if we faint not.
Galatians 6:9

Whatever your hand finds to do, do it with your might.
Ecclesiastes 9:10
NKJV

If a task is once begun, never leave it till it's done. Be the labor great or small, do it well or not at all.

Great minds have purpose; others have wishes.

"For I know the plans I have for you," declares the Lord, "plans to prosper you...to give you a hope and a future."
Jeremiah 29:11 NIV

Even when walking through the dark valley of death I will not be afraid, for you are close beside me, guarding, guiding all the way.

Psalm 23:4 TLB

I would rather walk with God in the dark than go alone in the light.

Laziness travels so slowly that poverty soon overtakes him.

Yet a little sleep, a little slumber, a little folding of the hands to sleep: so shall thy poverty come as one that travelleth; and thy want as an armed man.
Proverbs 24:33-34

For what is your life? It is even a vapor that appears for a little time and then vanishes away.

James 4:14 NKJV

Life is a coin. You can spend it any way you wish, but you can only spend it once.

You can accomplish
more in one hour
with God than
in one lifetime
without Him.

Walk in wisdom...
redeeming
the time.
Colossians 4:5

*For whatever
is born of God
overcomes the
world; and this
is the victory that
has overcome
the world —
our faith.*
1 John 5:4 NASB

Experience is not
what happens to a
man, it's what a man
does with what
happens to him.

Remember the difference between a boss and a leader: a boss says "Go!" — a leader says "Let's go!"

～

Let us go up at once, and possess it; for we are well able to overcome it.
Numbers 13:30

Life can't give me joy and peace; it's up to me to will it. Life just gives me time and space; it's up to me to fill it.

I have set before you life and death, the blessing and the curse; therefore choose life, that you and your descendants may live.
Deuteronomy 30:19 AMP

The size of your success is determined by the size of your belief.

Everything is possible for him who believes.

Mark 9:23 NIV

I press toward the goal for the prize of the upward call of God in Christ Jesus.

Philippians 3:14

NKJV

Destiny is not a matter of chance, it is a matter of choice. It is not a thing to be waited for; it is a thing to be achieved.

Man cannot discover new oceans unless he has the courage to lose sight of the shore.

Now the just shall live by faith: but if any man draw back, my soul shall have no pleasure in him.
Hebrews 10:38

A wise man will hear and increase in learning, And a man of understanding will acquire wise counsel.

Proverbs 1:5 NASB

I think the one lesson I have learned is that there is no substitute for paying attention.

Begin to act boldly. The moment one definitely commits oneself, heaven moves in his behalf.

Let us therefore come boldly unto the throne of grace, that we may obtain mercy, and find grace to help in time of need.

Hebrews 4:16

Righteous lips are the delight of kings; and they love him that speaketh right.
Proverbs 16:13

Protect your own credibility. One of the highest accolades is the comment, "If he says so, you can bank on it."

Our days are identical suitcases — all the same size — but some people can pack more into them than others.

Making the most of your time...
Ephesians 5:16
NASB

Where there is no vision, the people perish.
Proverbs 29:18

In life, as in football, you won't go far unless you know where the goal posts are.

Success is the result
of working hard,
playing hard,
and keeping your
mouth shut.

*Even a fool is
thought to be wise
when he is silent.
It pays him to keep
his mouth shut.*
Proverbs 17:28 TLB

My little children, let us not love in word, neither in tongue; but in deed and in truth.

1 John 3:18

People may doubt what you say, but they will believe what you do.

Never, never be too proud to say, "I'm sorry," to your child when you've made a mistake.

Confess your faults one to another, and pray one for another.
James 5:16

Before I (God) formed thee in the belly I knew thee; and before thou camest forth out of the womb I sanctified thee, and I ordained thee.

Jeremiah 1:5

There's a time when you have to explain to your children why they're born, and it's a marvelous thing if you know the reason.

Simply having children does not make mothers.

Teach the young women to be sober...to love their children.
Titus 2:4

Give, and it will be given to you...For by your standard of measure it will be measured to you in return.
Luke 6:38 NASB

Loving a child is a circular business... the more you give, the more you get, the more you get, the more you give.

Parents must get across the idea that, "I love you always, but sometimes I do not love your behavior."

Those whom I love, I reprove and discipline; be zealous therefore, and repent.
Revelation 3:19
NASB

*Behold,
children
are a gift
of the Lord.
Psalm 127:3 NASB*

Children are God's apostles, day by day sent forth to preach of love and hope and peace.

A child is fed with milk and praise.

~

Let no corrupt communication proceed out of your mouth, but that which is good to the use of edifying, that it may minister grace unto the hearers. Ephesians 4:29

Humble your-selves in the sight of the Lord, and he shall lift you up.

James 4:10

You are never so high as when you are on your knees.

Never despair of a child. The one you weep the most for at the mercy-seat may fill your heart with the sweetest joys.

He that goeth forth and weepeth, bearing precious seed, shall doubtless come again with rejoicing.
Psalm 126:6

And she conceived ...and said, I have gotten a man from the Lord.
Genesis 4:1

Babies are such a nice way to start people.

(Encouragement)
is the art of "turning
your children on,"
helping them do
for themselves,
not doing for them.

*And thou shalt
teach them
ordianances and
laws, and shalt
show them the way
wherein they must
walk, and the work
that they must do.
Exodus 18:20*

And be ye kind one to another, tenderhearted, forgiving one another, even as God for Christ's sake hath forgiven you.
Ephesians 4:32

"I can forgive, but I cannot forget," is only another way of saying, "I will not forgive." Forgiveness ought to be like a canceled note — torn in two, and burned up, so that it never can be shown against one.

If you have no prayer life yourself, it is rather a useless gesture to make your child say his prayers every night.

Pray without ceasing.
1 Thessalonians 5:17

First take the beam out of your own eye, and then you will see clearly to take out the speck that is in your brother's eye.

Luke 6:42 AMP

If there is anything we wish to change in the child, we should first examine it and see whether it is not something that could be better changed in ourselves.

Any child will learn to worship God who lives his daily life with adults who worship Him.

He who walks with the wise grows wise.
Proverbs 13:20 NIV

*(Love)...
believeth
all things,
hopeth
all things,
endureth
all things.*

1 Corinthians 13:7

My mother said to me, "If you become a soldier you'll be a general; if you become a monk you'll end up as the pope." Instead, I became a painter and wound up as Picasso.

Happy is the child...who sees mother and father rising early, or going aside regularly, to keep times with the Lord.

∽

Let the heart of them rejoice that seek the Lord. Seek the Lord, and his strength: seek his face evermore.

Psalm 105:3-4

If any of you lack wisdom, let him ask of God, that giveth to all men liberally, and upbraideth not; and it shall be given him.

James 1:5

I remember leaving the hospital... thinking, "Wait, are they going to let me just walk off with him? I don't know beans about babies!"

As a mother, my job is to take care of the possible and trust God with the impossible.

And they that know thy name will put their trust in thee: for thou, Lord, hast not forsaken them that seek thee.
Psalm 9:10

Let the wise listen.

Proverbs 1:5 NIV

If we as parents are too busy to listen to our children, how then can they understand a God who hears?

A mother once asked a clergyman when she should begin the education of her child,... "Madam," was the reply,... "From the very first smile that gleams over an infant's cheek, your opportunity begins."

Train up a child in the way he should go, Even when he is old he will not depart from it.
Proverbs 22:6 NASB

For the commandment is a lamp; and the law is light; and reproofs of instruction are the way of life.
Proverbs 6:23

If it is desirable that children be kind, appreciative, and pleasant, those qualities should be taught — not hoped for.

Through the ages
no nation has had
a better friend
than the mother
who taught her
child to pray.

*Devote yourselves
to prayer, keeping
alert in it with
an attitude of
thanksgiving.
Colossians 4:2
NASB*

*It is more
blessed
to give than
to receive.*

Acts 20:35

A mother is a person
who sees that there
are only four pieces
of pie for five persons
and promptly remarks
that she's never
cared for pie.

A mother is not a person to lean on, but a person to make leaning unnecessary.

Therefore shall a man leave his father and his mother, and shall cleave unto his wife: and they shall be one flesh.
Genesis 2:24

Her children arise up, and call her blessed; her husband also, and he praiseth her.

Proverbs 31:28

Of all the rights of women, the greatest is to be a mother.

A mother understands what a child does not say.

Serve him with a perfect heart and with a willing mind: for the Lord searcheth all hearts, and understandeth all the imaginations of the thoughts.
1 Chronicles 28:9

Correct thy son, and he shall give thee rest; yea, he shall give delight unto thy soul.

Proverbs 29:17

The persons hardest to convince they're at the retirement age are children at bedtime.

Motherhood is a partnership with God.

For this child I prayed; and the Lord hath given me my petition which I asked of him. Therefore also I have lent him to the Lord; as long as he liveth he shall be lent to the Lord.

1 Samuel 1:27-28

Her candle goeth not out by night.
Proverbs 31:18

A man's work is from sun to sun, but a mother's work is never done.

The more a child becomes aware of a mother's willingness to listen, the more a mother will begin to hear.

A wise man will hear, and will increase learning; and a man of understanding shall attain unto wise counsels.
Proverbs 1:5

But test every-thing that is said to be sure it is true, and if it is, then accept it.

1 Thessalonians 5:21 TLB

Fingerprinting children is a good idea. It will settle the question as to who used the guest towel in the bathroom.

Home, sweet home — where each lives for the other, and all live for God.

For none of us lives to himself alone and none of us dies to himself alone. If we live, we live to the Lord; and if we die, we die to the Lord. So, whether we live or die, we belong to the Lord.
Romans 14:7-8 NIV

The school will teach children how to read, but the environment of the home must teach them what to read. The school can teach them how to think, but the home must teach them what to believe.

Teach a child to choose the right path, and when he is older he will remain upon it.

Proverbs 22:6 TLB

Your children learn
more of your faith
during the bad times
than they do during
the good times.

*Consider it all joy,
my brethren, when
you encounter
various trials.*
James 1:2 NASB

The Lord is on my side; I will not fear: what can man do unto me?
Psalm 118:6

A woman who can cope with the terrible twos can cope with anything.

A little boy, age eight, gave a profound definition of parenthood: "Parents are just baby-sitters for God."

I prayed for this child, and the Lord has granted me what I asked of him. So now I give him to the Lord. For his whole life he will be given over to the Lord.

1 Samuel 1:27-28

NIV

A merry heart doeth good like a medicine.
Proverbs 17:22

Any time a child can be seen but not heard, it's a shame to wake him.

The quickest way for a parent to get a child's attention is to sit down and look comfortable.

A merry heart doeth good like a medicine.

Proverbs 17:22

There is a right time for every- thing: A time to laugh... Ecclesiastes 3:1,4 TLB

Parents of teens and parents of babies have something in common. They spend a great deal of time trying to get their kids to talk.

Every job is a self-portrait of the person who does it. Autograph your work with excellence.

Daniel was preferred above the presidents and princes, because an excellent spirit was in him.
Daniel 6:3

After this manner therefore pray ye...Thy kingdom come. Thy will be done in earth, as it is in heaven.

Matthew 6:9-10

Don't ask God for what you think is good; ask Him for what He thinks is good for you.

The wise does at once what the fool does at last.

He that gathereth in summer is a wise son: but he that sleepeth in harvest is a son that causeth shame.
Proverbs 10:5

Love endures long and is patient and kind...it takes no account of the evil done to it [it pays no attention to a suffered wrong].
1 Corinthians 13:4,5
AMP

Love sees through a telescope not a microscope.

Learn by experience — preferably other people's.

All these things happened to them as examples — as object lessons to us — to warn us against doing the same things.
1 Corinthians 10:11 TLB

*If thou faint
in the day of
adversity, thy
strength is small.
Proverbs 24:10*

Adversity causes
some men to
break; others
to break records.

To love what you do and feel that it matters — how could anything be more fun?

For my heart rejoiced in all my labour.
Ecclesiastes 2:10

He becometh poor that dealeth with a slack hand: but the hand of the diligent maketh rich.

Proverbs 10:4

There is no poverty that can overtake diligence.

What you do speaks so loud that I cannot hear what you say.

Show me your faith without deeds, and I will show you my faith by what I do.

James 2:18 NIV

For the weapons of our warfare are not carnal, but mighty through God to the pulling down of strongholds.

2 Corinthians 10:4

Prayer is an invisible tool which is wielded in a visible world.

No plan is worth the paper it is printed on unless it starts you doing something.

But be ye doers of the word, and not hearers only, deceiving your own selves.

James 1:22

*With God all
things are
possible.
Matthew 19:26*

Most of the things worth doing in the world had been declared impossible before they were done.

Diligence is
the mother of
good fortune.

*The plans of
the diligent
lead to profit.*
Proverbs 21:5 NIV

I keep under my body, and bring it into subjection.

1 Corinthians 9:27

I count him braver who overcomes his desires than him who conquers his enemies; for the hardest victory is the victory over self.

Vision is the world's most desperate need. There are no hopeless situations, only people who think hopelessly.

Where there is no vision, the people perish.
Proverbs 29:18

Pride only breeds quarrels, but wisdom is found in those who take advice.

Proverbs 13:10

NIV

Many receive advice, only the wise profit by it.

The greedy search for money or success will almost always lead men in to unhappiness. Why? Because that kind of life makes them depend upon things outside themselves.

Let your character be free from the love of money, being content with what you have; for He Himself has said, "I will never desert you nor will I ever forsake you."
Hebrews 13:5 NASB

For I have learned, in whatsoever state I am, therewith to be content. I can do all things through Christ which strengtheneth me.
Philippians 4:11,13

The happiest people don't necessarily have the best of everything. They just make the best of everything.

It's not hard to make decisions when you know what your values are.

But Daniel purposed in his heart that he would not defile himself.
Daniel 1:8

*He becometh poor
that dealeth with
a slack hand:
but the hand
of the diligent
maketh rich.*

Proverbs 10:4

When I was a young
man I observed that
nine out of ten things
I did were failures.
I didn't want to be a
failure, so I did ten
times more work.

Jumping to conclusions is not half as good an exercise as digging for facts.

Study to shew thyself approved unto God, a workman that needeth not to be ashamed, rightly dividing the word of truth.
2 Timothy 2:15

Let us lay aside every weight, and the sin which doth so easily beset us, and let us run with patience the race that is set before us.

Hebrews 12:1

Laziness is often mistaken for patience.

Every man is enthusiastic at times. One man has enthusiasm for thirty minutes, another has it for thirty days — but it is the man that has it for thirty years who makes a success in life.

~

Let us run with
perseverance
the race marked
out for us.
Hebrews 12:1 NIV

A good man out of the good treasure of the heart bringeth forth good things: and an evil man out of the evil treasure bringeth forth evil things.

Matthew 12:35

A man never discloses his own character so clearly as when he describes another's.

What we do on some great occasion will probably depend on what we already are; and what we are will be the result of previous years of self-discipline.

But I keep under my body, and bring it into subjection.
1 Corinthians 9:27

Finally, brethren, whatsoever things are true, whatsoever things are honest, whatsoever things are just...if there be any virtue, and if there be any praise, think on these things.

Philippians 4:8

A well-trained memory is one that permits you to forget everything that isn't worth remembering.

Blessed is the man who is too busy to worry in the daytime and too sleepy to worry at night.

The sleep of a labouring man is sweet.
Ecclesiastes 5:12

For ye have need of patience, that, after ye have done the will of God, ye might receive the promise.
Hebrews 10:36

Patience is bitter but its fruit is sweet.

When you are laboring for others let it be with the same zeal as if it were for yourself.

Each of you should look not only to your own interests, but also to the interests of others.

Philippians 2:4 NIV

He becometh poor that dealeth with a slack hand: but the hand of the diligent maketh rich.

Proverbs 10:4

When you do the things you have to do when you have to do them, the day will come when you can do the things you want to do when you want to do them.

A man without mirth is like a wagon without springs, he is jolted disagreeably by every pebble in the road.

A merry heart doeth good like a medicine: but a broken spirit drieth the bones.
Proverbs 17:22

Am I now trying to win the approval of men or of God?
Galatians 1:10
NIV

I don't know the secret to success but the key to failure is to try to please everyone.

References

Unless otherwise indicated, all scripture quotations are taken from the *King James Version* of the Bible.

Scripture quotations marked NIV are taken from the *Holy Bible, New International Version* ®. NIV ®. Copyright © 1973, 1978, 1984 by International Bible Society. Used by permission of Zondervan Publishing House. All rights reserved.

Verses marked ICB are taken from the *International Children's Bible,* New Century Version. Copyright © 1986, 1988 by Word Publishing, Dallas, TX 75039. Used by permission.

Scripture quotations marked TLB are taken from *The Living Bible,* copyright © 1971. Used by permission of Tyndale House Publishers, Inc., Wheaton, Illinois 60189. All rights reserved.

Verses marked NASB are taken from the *New American Standard Bible.* Copyright © The Lockman Foundation 1960, 1962, 1963, 1968, 1971, 1972, 1973, 1975, 1977. Used by permission.

Scripture quotations marked AMP are taken from *The Amplified Bible. Old Testament* copyright ©1965, 1987 by Zondervan Corporation. *New Testament* copyright © 1958, 1987 by the Lockman Foundation. Used by permission.

Verses marked NKJV are taken from *The New King James Version* of the Bible. Copyright © 1979, 1980, 1982, 1994 by Thomas Nelson, Inc., Publishers. Used by permission.

Scripture quotation marked NRSV is taken from the *New Revised Standard Version Bible,* copyright ©1989 by the Division of Christian Education of the Churches of Christ in the United States of America and is used by permission.

Acknowledgments

We acknowledge and thank the following people for the quotes used in this book: Calvin Coolidge (5), Gary Smalley & John Trent (6), John A. Shedd (7,245), Ed Cole (8,292), Helen Keller (9), John Sculley (10), Thomas A. Edison (12), Winston Churchill (13), Hannah More (14), Harry Emerson Fosdick (15), Wilson Mizner (16), Witt Fowler (17), Bill Copeland (18), Les Brown (19), Dr. Eugene Swearingen (20), Thomas Jefferson (21,26), Ken Hubbard (22), Ralph Waldo Emerson (23,209,291), Solon (25,290), William James (27), Ronald E. Osborn (28), Bacon (29), Orlando A. Battista (30,308), Mark Twain (31,101,109,212,214), George Sala (32), Josh McDowell (34), Dan Bennett (36), Richard Dobbins (38), Thomas Kempis (39), Ruth Bell Graham (40,261), Glen Wheeler (43,69,265,279), Odgen Nash (44), George Adams (55), Mignon McLaughlin (58), Bishop Jeremy Taylor (59), Maria Lovell (62), James Dobson (64,68,82,87,94,97,264), Martin Luther (65), Howard & Jeanne Hendricks (66), Tim Hansel (70), Abraham Lincoln (71), Sara Gilbert (72), David Shibley (73), Dr. Anthony Witham (74,89), Terence (75), General Douglas MacArthur (77), R. Kent Hughes (78), Alan Beck (79), Kathryn McCarthy Graham (81,289), Henry Ward Beecher (83,85,91, 254,313), Harold S. Hulbert (84), Paul Lewis (88), David Jeremiah (90), M. Scott Peck (92), Bill Cosby (93,314), Gordon MacDonald (95), Don Marquis (96), Mencuis (98), Hugh Prather (99), Robert C. Savage (100), Paul Harvey (102), Freeman (103), Doug Larson (104), J. Hudson Taylor (105),

Norman Vincent Peale (106), C. Everett Koop (107), Waterloo (110), Thomas Chandler Haliburton (114), Charles Spurgeon (115), C.L. Wheeler (117), Fanuel Tjingaete (118), Dwight L. Moody (119), Malcolm Smith (120), Booker T. Washington (122), Ken S. Keyes, Jr. (123), Richard Exley (126), A.W. Tozer (127), Robert Orben (131), Michael LeBouef (132), Alphonse Karr (134), Olin Miller (135), Dwight D. Eisenhower (136), John D. Rockefeller, Jr. (207), Zig Ziglar (208,312), Friedrich Wilhelm Nietzche (210), Diane Ravitch (211), a Jesuit motto (216), Jim Rohn (219), Michael Asper (220), Woodrow Wilson (221), Richard Nixon (223), Washington Irving (225), Mary Gardiner Brainard (226), Benjamin Franklin (227), Lillian Dickson (228), James Huxley (230), E.M. Kelly (231), David J. Schwartz (233), William Jennings Bryan (234), Diane Sawyer (236), Johann Wolfgang von Goethe (237), James L. Hayes (238), Arnold Glasow (240), Albert Einstein (241), Hazel Scot (244), Penelope Leach (246), Amy Vanderbilt (247), Lowell (248), Mary Lamb (249), Jean Hodges (250), T.L. Cuyler (251), Don Herold (252), Dr. William Mitchell & Dr. Charles Paul Conn (253), Peter Marshall (255), C.G. Jung (256), Anna B. Mow (257), Pablo Picasso (259), Anne Tyler (260), V. Gilbert Beers (262), Whatley (263), Dorothy Canfield Fisher (267), Lin Yutang (268), Jewish proverb (269), Shannon Fife (270), T.J. Bach (275), Charles A. Wells (276), Beverly LaHaye (277), Judith Clabes (278), Paul Swets (280), Lane Olinhouse (281), William A. Ward (288), William H. Danforth (293), Louis D. Brandeis (294), Cervantes (295), Aristotle (296), Winifred Newman (297), Syrus (298), Andre Maurois (299), Roy Disney (301), George Bernard Shaw (302), Jean Paul Richter (306), H.P. Liddon (307), Phil Marquart (309).

Additional copies of this book and other titles in the *God's Little Instruction Book* Series are available at your local bookstore.

God's Little Instruction Book
God's Little Instruction Book II
God's Little Instruction Book for Mom
God's Little Instruction Book for Dad
God's Little Instruction Book for Graduates
God's Little Instruction Book for Students
God's Little Instruction Book for Kids
God's Little Instruction Book for Couples
God's Little Instruction Book for Men
God's Little Instruction Book for Women
God's Little Instruction Book Daily Calendar

HONOR
B O O K S

Tulsa, Oklahoma